ReadyGEN™

GRADE **3**

Start of the Year
STUDENT MATERIALS

PEARSON

Glenview, Illinois • Boston, Massachusetts • Chandler, Arizona • Upper Saddle River, New Jersey

ISBN-13: 978-0-328-78893-4
ISBN-10:   0-328-78893-7
1 2 3 4 5 6 7 8 9 10 V063 17 16 15 14 13

Table of Contents

Unit 1 Observing the World Around Us

Text Collections

Sleuth

Reader's and Writer's Journal

Module A

Module B

Text Collections

thunder cake

PATRICIA POLACCO

On sultry summer days at my grandma's farm in Michigan, the air gets damp and heavy. Stormclouds drift low over the fields. Birds fly close to the ground. The clouds glow for an instant with a sharp, crackling light, and then a roaring, low, tumbling sound of thunder makes the windows shudder in their panes. The sound used to scare me when I was little. I loved to go to Grandma's house (Babushka, as I used to call my grandma, had come from Russia years before), but I feared Michigan's summer storms. I feared the sound of thunder more than anything. I always hid under the bed when the storm moved near the farmhouse.

This is the story of how my grandma—my Babushka—helped me overcome my fear of thunderstorms.

Grandma looked at the horizon, drew a deep breath and said, "This is Thunder Cake baking weather, all right. Looks like a storm coming to me."

"Child, you come out
from under that bed. It's
only thunder you're hearing,"
my grandma said.

The air was hot, heavy
and damp. A loud clap of
thunder shook the house,
rattled the windows and
made me grab her close.

"Steady, child, she cooed.
"Unless you let go of me,
we won't be able to make a
Thunder Cake today!"

"Thunder Cake?" I stammered as I hugged her even closer.

"Don't pay attention to that old thunder, except to see how close the storm is getting. When you see the lightning, start counting…real slow. When you hear the thunder, stop counting. That number is how many miles away the storm is. Understand?" she asked. "We need to know how far away the storm is, so we have time to make the cake and get it into the oven before the storm comes, or it won't be real Thunder Cake."

7

Her eyes surveyed the black clouds a way off in the distance. Then she strode into the kitchen. Her worn hands pulled a thick book from the shelf above the woodstove.

"Let's find that recipe, child," she crowed as she lovingly fingered the grease-stained pages to a creased spot.

"Here it is…Thunder Cake!"

She carefully penned the ingredients on a piece of notepaper. " Now let's gather all the things we'll need!" she exclaimed as she scurried toward the back door.

We were by the barn door when a huge bolt of lightning flashed. I started counting, like grandma told me to, "1-2-3-4-5-6-7-8-9-10."

Then the thunder ROARED!

"Ten miles… it's ten miles away," Grandma said as she looked at the sky. "About an hour away, I'd say. You'll have to hurry, child. Gather them eggs careful-like," she said

Eggs from mean old Nellie Peck Hen. I was scared. I knew she would try to peck me.

"I'm here, she won't hurt you. Just get them eggs," Grandma said softly.

The lightning flashed again. "1-2-3-4-5-6-7-8-9" I counted.

"Nine miles," Grandma reminded me.

Milk was next. Milk from old Kick Cow. As Grandma milked her, Kick Cow turned and looked mean, right at me. I was scared. She looked so big.

Zip went the lightning. "1-2-3-4-5-6-7-8," I counted. BAROOOOOOOOM went the thunder.

"Eight miles, child," Grandma croaked. "Now we have to get chocolate and sugar and flour from the dry shed."

I was scared as we walked down the path from the farmhouse through Tangleweed Woods to the dry shed. Suddenly the lightning slit the sky!

"1-2-3-4-5-6-7" I counted. BOOOOOOM BA-BOOOOOOM, crashed the thunder. It scared me a lot, but I kept walking with Grandma.

Another jagged edge of lightning flashed as I crept into the dry shed! "1-2-3-4-5-6" I counted. CRACKLE, CRACKLE BOOOOOOOM, KA-BOOOOOM, the thunder bellowed. It was dark and I was scared.

"I'm here, child," Grandma said softly from the doorway. "Hurry now, we haven't got much time. We've got everything but the secret ingredient."

"Three overripe tomatoes and some strawberries," Grandma whispered as she squinted at the list.

I climbed up high on the trellis. The ground looked a long way down. I was scared.

"I'm here, child," she said. Her voice was steady and soft. "You won't fall."

I reached three luscious tomatoes while she picked strawberries. Lightning again!

"1-2-3-4-5" I counted.

KA-BANG BOOOOOOOOOAROOOOOM, the thunder growled.

We hurried back to the house and the warm kitchen, and we measured the ingredients. I poured them into the mixing bowl while Grandma mixed. I churned butter for the frosting and melted chocolate. Finally, we poured the batter into the cake pans and put them into the oven together.

Lightning lit the kitchen! I only counted to three and the thunder RRRRUMBLED and CRASHED.

"Three miles away," Grandma said, "and the cake is in the oven. We made it! We'll have a real Thunder Cake!"

As we waited for the cake, Grandma looked out the window for a long time. "Why, you aren't afraid of thunder. You're too brave!" she said as she looked right at me.

"I'm not brave, Grandma," I said. "I was under the bed! Remember?"

"But you got out from under it," she answered, "and you got eggs from mean old Nellie Peck Hen, you got milk from old Kick Cow, you went through Tangleweed Woods to the dry shed, you climbed the trellis in the barnyard. From where I sit, only a very brave person could have done all them things!"

19

I thought and thought as the storm rumbled closer. She was right. I was brave!

"Brave people can't be afraid of a sound, child," she said as we spread out the tablecloth and set the table. When we were done, we hurried into the kitchen to take the cake out of the oven. After the cake had cooled, we frosted it.

Just then the lightning flashed, and this time it lit the whole sky. Even before the last flash had faded, the thunder ROLLED, BOOOOOMED, CRASHED, and BBBBAAAAARRRRROOOOOOOOMMMMMMMMMED just above us. The storm was here!

"Perfect," Grandma cooed, "just perfect." She beamed as she added the last strawberry to the glistening chocolate frosting on top of our Thunder Cake.

As rain poured down on our roof, Grandma cut a wedge for each of us. She poured us steaming cups of tea from the samovar.

When the thunder ROARED above us so hard it shook the windows and rattled the dishes in the cupboards, we just smiled and ate our Thunder Cake.

From that time on, I never feared the voice of thunder again.

The Lemonade War

by Jacqueline Davies

Location, Location, Location

Evan Treski and his younger sister Jessie are in a contest to see who can earn $100 selling lemonade by Saturday. So far Jessie is winning.

Evan was in trouble. So far, he'd earned forty-seven dollars and eleven cents, which was more money than he'd ever had in his whole life. But today was Friday. There were only three days left. Three days to beat Jessie. He needed to earn almost fifty-three dollars to win the bet. And that meant each day he had to earn—

Evan tried to do the math in his head. Fifty-three divided by three. Fifty-three divided by three. His brain spun like a top. He didn't know where to begin.

He went to his desk, pulled out a piece of paper— his basketball schedule from last winter— and flipped it over to the back. He found the stub of a pencil in his bottom desk drawer, and on the paper he wrote

$$53 \div 3 =$$

He stared and stared at the equation on the page. The number fifty-three was just too big. He didn't know how to do it.

"Jessie would know how," he muttered, scribbling hard on the page. Jessie could do long division. Jessie had her multiplication facts memorized all the way up to fourteen times fourteen. Jessie would look at a problem like this and just do it in her head. *Snap*.

Evan felt his mouth getting tight, his fingers gripping the pencil too hard, as he scribbled a dark storm cloud on the page. His math papers from school were always covered in X's. Nobody else got as many X's as he did. Nobody.

Draw a picture. Mrs. DeFazio's voice floated in his head. She had always reminded him to draw a picture when he couldn't figure out how to start a math problem. A picture of what? he asked in his head. Anything?

Yes, anything, as long as there are fifty-three of them.

Dollar signs. Evan decided to draw dollar signs. He started to draw three rows of dollar signs. "One, two, three," he counted, as he drew:

$
$
$

"Four, five, six." He drew:

$ $
$ $
$ $

By the time he reached fifty-three, his page looked like this:

$ $ $ $ $ $ $ $ $ $ $ $ $ $ $ $ $

$ $ $ $ $ $ $ $ $ $ $ $ $ $ $ $ $

$ $ $ $ $ $ $ $ $ $ $ $ $ $ $ $ $

There were seventeen dollar signs in each row. And then those two extra dollar signs left over. Evan drew a ring around those two extras.

$ $ $ $ $ $ $ $ $ $ $ $ $ $ $ $ $ ⟨$⟩

$ $ $ $ $ $ $ $ $ $ $ $ $ $ $ $ $ ⟨$⟩

$ $ $ $ $ $ $ $ $ $ $ $ $ $ $ $ $

Seventeen dollar signs. And two left over.

Evan stared at the picture for a long time. He wrote "Friday" next to the first row, "Saturday" next to the second row, and "Sunday" next to the third row.

Friday $ $ $ $ $ $ $ $ $ $ $ $ $ $ $ $ $ ⟨$⟩

Saturday $ $ $ $ $ $ $ $ $ $ $ $ $ $ $ $ $ ⟨$⟩

Sunday $ $ $ $ $ $ $ $ $ $ $ $ $ $ $ $ $

Evan looked at the picture. It started to make sense. He needed to make seventeen dollars on Friday, seventeen dollars on Saturday, and seventeen dollars on Sunday. And somewhere over the three days, he needed to make two *extra* bucks in order to earn fifty-three dollars by Sunday evening.

Evan felt his heart jump in his chest. He had done it. He had figured out fifty-three divided by three. That was a fourth-grade problem. That was *fourth-grade* math. And he hadn't even started *fourth-grade!* And no one had helped him. Not Mom, not Grandma, not Jessie. He'd done it all by himself. It was like shooting the winning basket in double overtime! He hadn't felt this good since the Lemonade War had begun.

But seventeen dollars a day? How was he going to do that? Yesterday he'd made forty-five dollars, but that was because he'd had help (and free supplies) from his friends. They weren't going to want to run a lemonade stand every day. Especially on the last days of summer vacation.

He needed a plan. Something that would guarantee good sales. The weather was holding out, that was for sure. It was going to hit 95 degrees today. A real scorcher. People would be thirsty, all right. Evan closed his eyes and imagined a crowd of thirsty people, all waving dollar bills at him. Now where was he going to find a lot of thirsty people with money to spend?

An idea popped into Evan's head. *Yep!* It was perfect. He just needed to find something with wheels to get him there.

It took Evan half an hour to drag his loaded wagon to the town center—a distance he usually traveled in less than five minutes by bike. But once he was there, he knew it was worth it.

It was lunchtime and the shaded benches on the town green were filled with people sprawling in the heat. Workers from the nearby stores on their half-hour lunch breaks, moms out with their kids, old people who didn't want to be cooped up in their houses all day. High school kids on skateboards slooshed by. Preschoolers climbed on the life-size sculpture of a circle of children playing ring-around-the-rosey. Dogs lay under trees, their tongues hanging out, *pant, pant, pant.*

Evan surveyed the scene and picked his spot, right in the center of the green where all the paths met. Anyone walking across the green would have to pass his stand. And who could resist lemonade on a day as hot as this?

But first he wheeled his wagon off to the side, parking it halfway under a huge rhododendron. Then he crossed the street and walked into the Big Dipper.

The frozen air felt good on his skin. It was like getting dunked in a vat of just-melted ice cream. And the smells—*mmmmmm*. A mix of vanilla, chocolate, coconut, caramel, and bubblegum. He looked at the tubs of ice cream, all in a row, carefully protected behind a pane of glass. The money in his pocket tingled. He had plenty left over after buying five cans of frozen lemonade mix with his earnings from yesterday. What would it hurt to buy just one cone? Or a milk shake? Or maybe both?

"Can I help you?" asked the woman behind the counter.

"Uh, yeah," said Evan. He stuck his hand in his pocket and felt all the money. BIlls and coins ruffled between his fingers. Money was meant to be spent. Why not spend a little?

"I, uh. . ." Evan could just imagine how good the ice cream would feel sliding down his hot throat. Creamy. Sweet. Like cold, golden deliciousness. He let his mind float as he gazed at the swirly buckets of ice cream.

The sound of laughter brought him back to earth in a hurry. He looked around. It was just some girls he didn't know at the water fountain. But it had *sounded* like Megan Moriarty.

"Can you please tell me how much a glass of lemonade costs?"

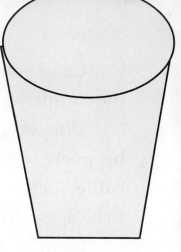

"Three dollars," said the woman.

"Really?" said Evan. "That much? How big's the cup?"

The woman pulled a plastic cup off a stack and held it up. It wasn't much bigger than the eight-ounce cups Evan had in his wagon.

"Wow. Three bucks. That's a lot," said Evan. "Well, thanks anyway." He started to walk to the door.

"Hey," said the woman, pointing to the ice cream case. "I'm allowed to give you a taste for free."

"Really?" said Evan. "Then, uh, could I taste the Strawberry Slam?" The woman handed him a tiny plastic spoon with three licks' worth of pink ice cream on it. Evan swallowed it all in one gulp. *Aahhh.*

Back outside, he got to work. First he filled his pitchers with water from the drinking fountain. Then he stirred in the mix. Then he pulled out a big blue marker and wrote on a piece of paper, "$2 per cup. Best price in town."

He'd barely finished setting up when the customers started lining up. And they didn't stop. For a full hour, he poured lemonade. *The world is a thirsty place,* he thought as he nearly emptied his fourth pitcher of the day. *And I am the Lemonade King.*

(Later, Evan would think of something his grandma said: "Pride goeth before a fall.")

When Evan looked up, there was Officer Ken, his hands on his hips, looking down on him. Evan gulped. He stared at the large holstered gun strapped to Officer Ken's belt.

"Hello," said Officer Ken, not smiling.

"Hi," said Evan. Officer Ken did the Bike Rodeo every year at Evan's school. He was also the cop who had shown up last fall when there was a hurt goose on the recess field. Officer Ken was always smiling. *Why isn't he smiling now?* Evan wondered.

"Do you have a permit?" asked Officer Ken. He had a very deep voice, even when he talked quietly, like he did now.

"You mean, like, a bike permit?" That's what the Rodeo was all about. If they passed the Rodeo, the third-graders got their bike permits, which meant they were allowed to ride to school.

"No. I mean a permit to sell food and beverages in a public space. You need to get a permit from the town hall. And pay a fee for the privilege."

Pay the town hall to run a lemonade stand? Was he kidding? Evan looked at Officer Ken's face. He didn't look like he was kidding.

"I didn't know I needed one," said Evan.

"Sorry, friend," said Officer Ken. "I'm going to have to shut you down. It's the law."

"But. . . but . . . there are lemonade stands all over town," said Evan. He thought of Jessie and Megan's lemonade stand. When he'd wheeled by with his wagon more than an hour ago, their stand had looked like a beehive, with small kids crowding around. He had read the sign over their stand: FREE FACE PAINTING! NAIL-POLISHING! HAIR- BRAIDING! What a gimmick! But it sure looked like it was working. "You know," said Evan, "there's a stand on Damon Road right now. You should go bust them."

Officer Ken smiled. "We tend to look the other way when it's in a residential neighborhood. But right here, on the town green, we have to enforce the law. Otherwise we'd have someone selling something every two feet."

"But—" There had to be some way to convince Officer Ken. How could Evan make him understand? "You see, I've got this little sister. And we've got a . . . a . . . competition going. To see who can sell the most lemonade. And I've *got* to win. Because she's . . . " He couldn't explain the rest. About fourth grade. And how embarrassed he was to be in the same class as his kid sister. And how it made him feel like a great big loser.

Evan looked up at Officer Ken. Officer Ken looked down at Evan. It was like Officer Ken was wearing a mask. A no-smiling, I'm-not-your-buddy mask.

Then Officer Ken shook his head and smiled and the mask feel off. " I've got a little sister, too," he said. "Love her to death, *now*, but when we were kids— Officer Ken sucked in his breath and shook his head again. *"Hooo!"*

Then the mask came back, and Officer Ken looked right at Evan for ten very stern seconds.

"Tell you what," said Officer Ken. " I *do* have to shut you down. The law's the law. But before I do, I'll buy one last glass of lemonade. How's that sound?"

Evan's face fell. "Sure," he said without enthusiasm. He poured an extra-tall cup and gave it to the policeman.

Officer Ken reached into his pocket and handed Evan a five dollar bill. "Keep the change," he said. "A contribution to the Big Brother Fund. Now clean up your things and don't leave any litter behind." He lifted his cup in a toast as he walked away.

Evan watched him go. *Wow,* he thought. *I just sold the most expensive cup of lemonade in town.*

Evan stared at the five-dollar bill in his hand.

It was funny. Two days ago he would have felt as rich as a king to have that money in his hands. It was enough to buy two slices of pizza and a soda with his friends. It was enough to rent a video and have a late night at someone's house. It was enough to buy a whole bagful of his favorite candy mix at CVS.

Two days ago, he would have been jumping for joy.

Now he looked at the five dollars and thought, *It's nothing*. Compared to the one hundred dollars he needed to win the war, five dollars was nothing. He felt somehow that he's been robbed of something— maybe the happiness he should have been feeling.

He loaded everything from his stand into the wagon, making sure he didn't leave a scrap of litter behind. He still had a glassful of lemonade left in one pitcher, not to mention another whole pitcher already mixed up and unsold, so he poured himself a full cup. Then, before beginning the long, hot haul back to his house, he found an empty spot on a shaded bench and pulled his earnings out of his pockets.

He counted once. He counted twice. Very slowly.

He had made sixty-five dollars. The cups and lemonade mix had cost nine dollars. When he added in his earnings from Wednesday and Thursday, he had one hundred and three dollars and eleven cents.

Now that's *enough*, he thought.

The MOON Seems to Change

by Franklyn M. Branley

Tonight take a look at the sky. See if the moon is there.

It may be big and round. It is a full moon.

FULL

Maybe you will see only part of it. It may be a quarter moon.

QUARTER

Or it may be only a little sliver. It is called a crescent moon.

CRESCENT

As the nights go by you can see changes in the moon. After the moon is full you see less and less of it. There are three or four nights with no moon at all. Then you see more and more of it. The moon seems to change

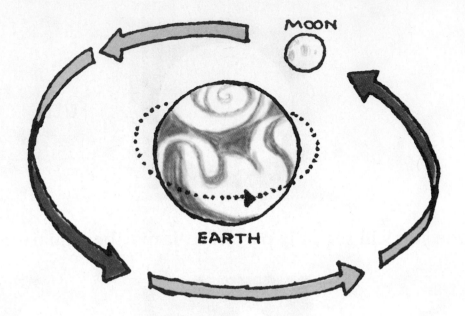

MOON

EARTH

It really doesn't. It seems to change because the moon goes around Earth. As it goes around, we see more of it— the moon gets bigger. It is a waxing moon. Or we see less of it—the moon gets smaller. It is a waning moon.

⇒— WAXING MOON →

⇒— WANING MOON →

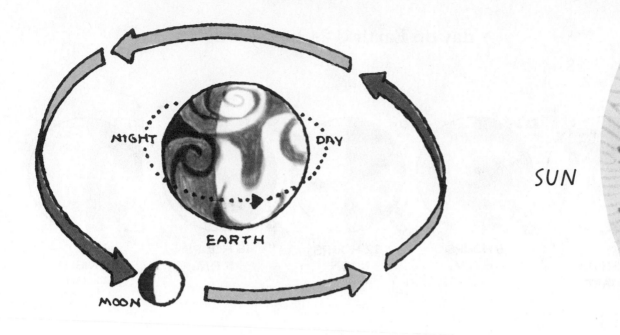

SUN

Half of the moon is always lighted by the sun. Half is lighted and half is always in darkness. It's the same with Earth. While one half of Earth is having sunshine and daylight, the other half is getting no sunshine. It is night.

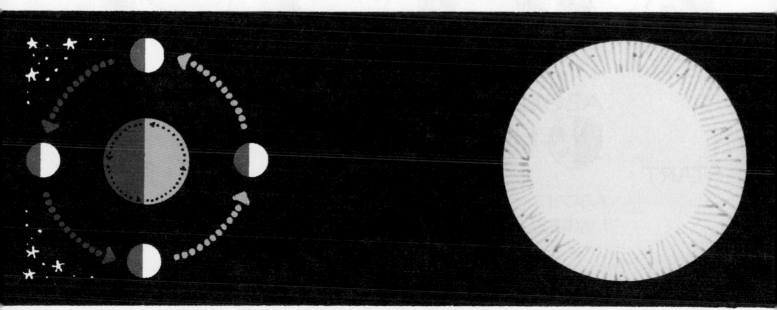

A day on Earth is 24 hours long.

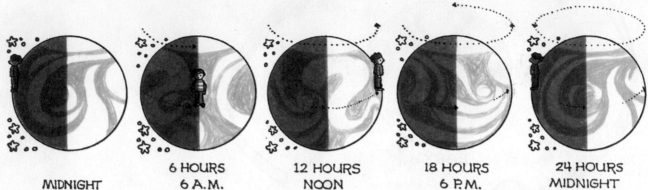

MIDNIGHT
START

6 HOURS
6 A.M.

12 HOURS
NOON

18 HOURS
6 P.M.

24 HOURS
MIDNIGHT
FINISH

A day on the moon
is almost a month long.

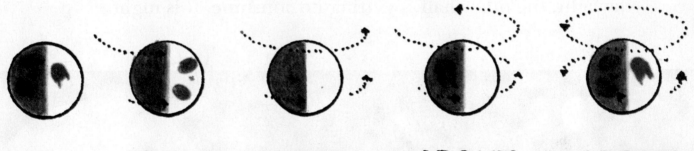

START

ABOUT
1 WEEK

ABOUT
2 WEEKS

ABOUT
3 WEEKS

ABOUT
4 WEEKS

FINISH

46

It takes the moon about
four weeks to go around Earth.

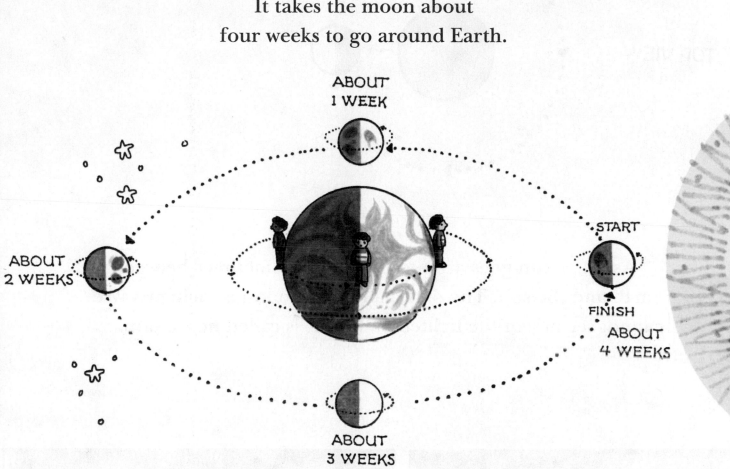

47

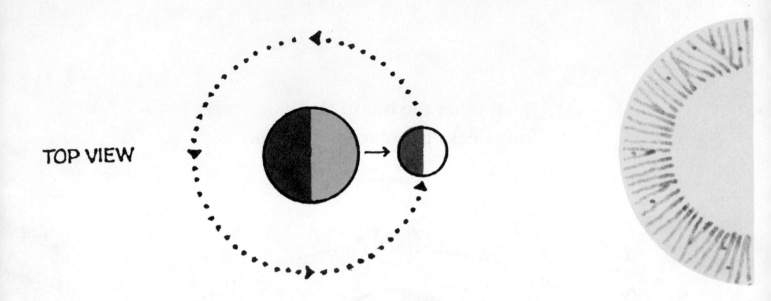

TOP VIEW

As the moon goes around Earth, it is sometimes between Earth and the sun. The dark half of the moon is facing us. We cannot see any of the lighted half. This is called new moon.

DARK SIDE OF MOON FACING US SO WE CANNOT SEE IT.

NEW MOON NOT IN NIGHT SKY SO WE CANNOT SEE IT.

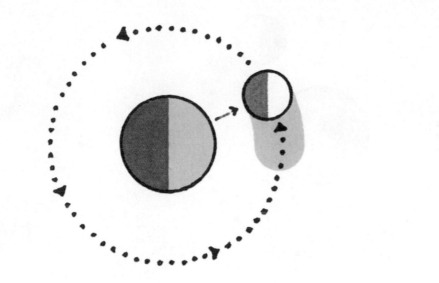

A night or two later the moon has moved a little bit along its path around Earth. We can then see a small part of the lighted half. It is called a crescent moon. We see it just after sunset. It is in the west, where we see the sun go down. You may be able to see it before the sky is dark. Sometimes you can see it in daytime.

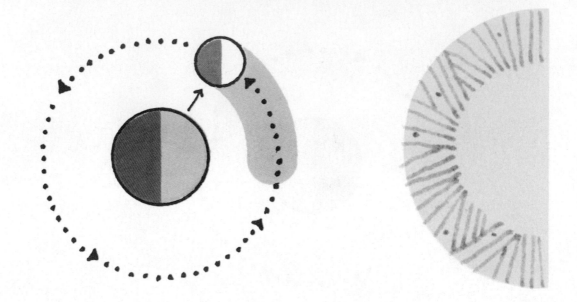

Each night the moon seems to grow. The moon is waxing.
We can see a bit more of the lighted half.

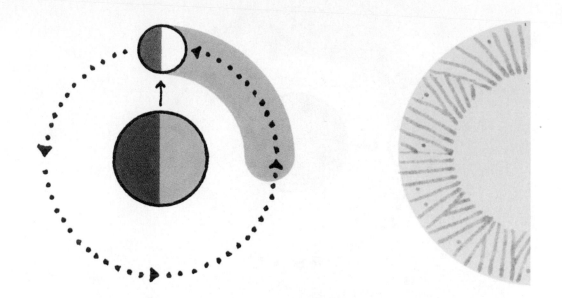

About a week after the moon is new, it has become a first-quarter moon. It looks like this. Sometimes you can see it in the afternoon before the sky is dark.

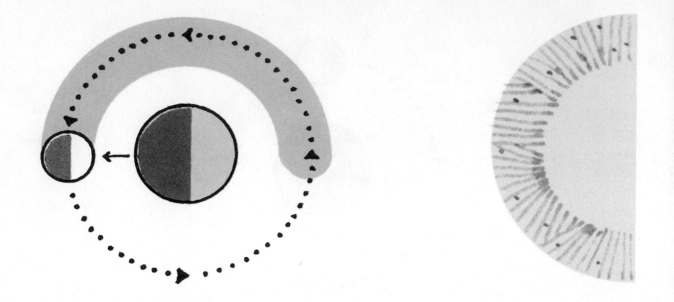

After another week the moon is on one side of Earth and the sun is on the other side. We can see all the lighted half of the moon. It is a full moon. We see it in the east as the sun sets in the west. We can't see it in the daytime.

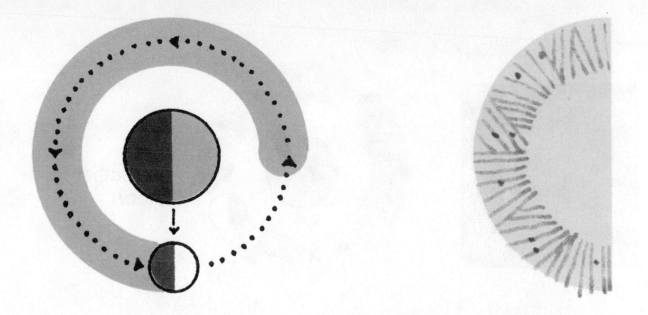

Each night after it is full, we see less and less of the moon. The moon is waning. In about a week it is a quarter moon. This is third quarter. It can be seen after midnight.

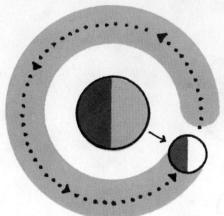

CRESCENT
MOON

After that, the moon once more becomes a crescent. Each night the crescent gets a bit thinner. We would see it later and later at night—long after we're usually asleep. A few days later we cannot see the moon at all. It is once again a new moon. About four weeks after the moon is new, we have another new moon.

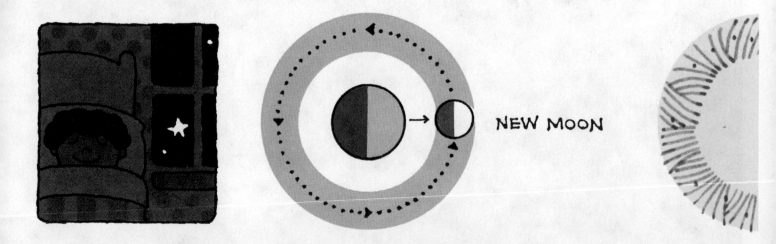

NEW MOON

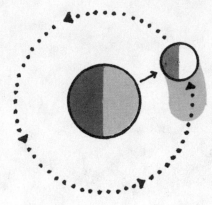
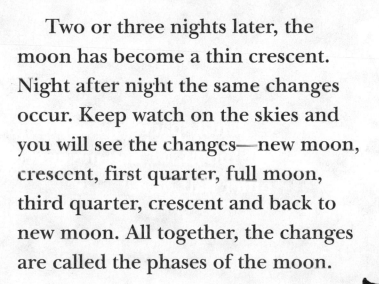

Two or three nights later, the moon has become a thin crescent. Night after night the same changes occur. Keep watch on the skies and you will see the changes— new moon, crescent, first quarter, full moon, third quarter, crescent and back to new moon. All together, the changes are called the phases of the moon.

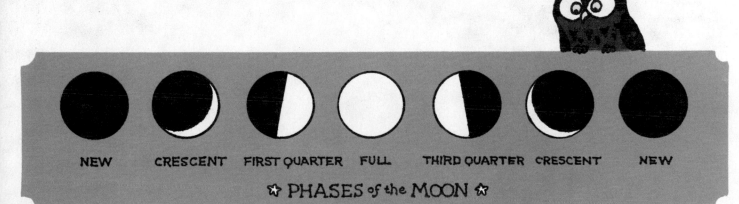

NEW   CRESCENT   FIRST QUARTER   FULL   THIRD QUARTER   CRESCENT   NEW

☆ PHASES of the MOON ☆

THIS IS THE SIDE
OF THE MOON
YOU CAN SEE
FROM THE EARTH

Until spaceships went around
the moon, we had never seen the
other half of it.

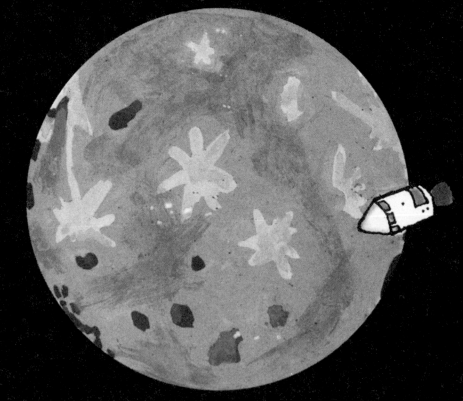

THE OTHER
SIDE

Sometimes we see a lot
of the part of the moon that
is turned toward us, and
sometimes only a little of it.
The moon grows bigger, and
then gets smaller. The moon
seems to change. It goes
through phases because it
goes around Earth.

Which phase of the moon can you see tonight?

NEW   CRESCENT   FIRST QUARTER   FULL   THIRD QUARTER   CRESCENT

Brother

by Mary Ann Hoberman

I had a little brother
And I brought him to my mother
And I said I want another
Little brother for a change.

But she said don't be a bother
So I took him to my father
And I said this little bother
Of a brother's very strange.

But he said one little brother
Is exactly like another
And every little brother
Misbehaves a bit he said.

So I took the little brother
From my mother and my father
And I put the little bother
Of a brother back to bed.

Magnifying Glass

by Valerie Worth

Small grains
In a stone
Grow edges
That twinkle;

The smooth
Moth's wing
Sprouts feathers
Like shingles;

My thumb
Is wrapped
In rich
Satin wrinkles

Rhyme

by Elizabeth Coatsworth

I like to see a thunder storm,
    A dunder storm,
      A blunder storm,
I like to see it, black and slow,
Come stumbling down the hills.

I like to hear a thunder storm,
    A plunder storm,
      A wonder storm,
Roar loudly at our little house
And shake the window sills!

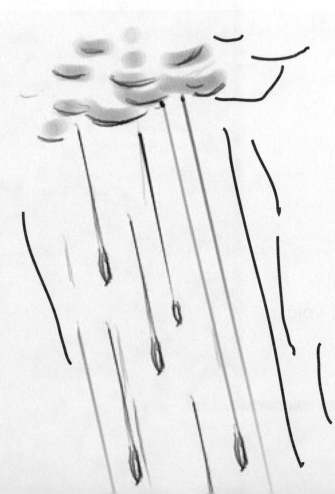

Roots

by Douglas Florian

The roots of trees
Don't just grow **d**
    o
    w
    n.

They **b r a n c h** out
Sideways, underground,

To help the tree to get a grip,
To anchor it so it won't slip.
As root hairs drink
The rain that **p**
    o
    u
    r
    s

They sip it up like tiny straws.
While by the growing roots in holes
Live badgers, rabbits, moles, and voles.
They tunnel under roots of trees
And root there for their families.

Under the Microscope
by Lee Bennett Hopkins

Unseen with
an unaided eye
amoebas
glide
on a small
glass slide.

Magnified
one thousand times
protozoans
split in two—

it's miraculous
what
a microscope
can do.

Summer Full Moon

by James Kirkup

The cloud tonight
is like a white
   Persian cat—

It lies among the stars
with eyes almost shut,
lapping the milk from
the moon's brimming dish.

The Moon is a White Cat

– from Hungary

The moon is a white cat
that hunts
the gray mice of night.

Acknowledgments

Text Credits

"Thunder Cake," by Patricia Polacco from *Thunder Cake.* Copyright © 1990 by Patricia Polacco. Used by permission of Philomel Books, A Division of Penguin Young Readers, A Member of Penguin Group (USA) Inc., 345 Hudson Street, New York, NY 10014. All rights reserved.

"The Lemonade Wars," Excerpt from *The Lemonade War* by Jacqueline Davis. Copyright © 2007 by Jacqueline Davis. Reprinted by arrangement with Houghton Mifflin Harcourt Publishing Company. All rights reserved.

"Rhyme," from *The Sparrow Bush* by Elizabeth Coatsworth, copyright © 1966 by Grosset & Dunlap, Inc., renewed. Used by permission of Grosset & Dunlap, Inc., a division of Penguin Group (USA) LLC.

"magnifying glass," From *All the Small Poems and Fourteen More.* Copyright © 1987 by Valerie Worth. Illustrations © by Natalie Babbitt. Reprinted by permission of Henry Holt & Company, LLC. All Rights Reserved.

"Brother," Used by permission of The Gina Maccoby Literary Agency. Copyright © 1959 by Mary Ann Hoberman.

"Brother," from *The Llama Who Had No Pajama: 100 Favorite Poems* by Mary Ann Hoberman. Text copyright © 1959 and renewed 1987 by Mary Ann Hoberman. Reprinted by permission of Houghton Mifflin Harcourt Publishing Company. All rights reserved.

"Under the Microscope," Copyright © 1999 by Lee Bennett Hopkins. First appeared in *Spectacular Science,* published by Simon & Schuster, Inc. Reprinted by permission of Curtis Brown, Ltd.

"The Moon Seems to Change," by Franklyn Branley, illustrations by Barbara Emberly and Ed Emberly, from *The Moon Seems to Change.* Text Copyright © 1987 by Franklyn Branley, illustrations © by Barbara Emberly and Ed Emberly. Used by permission of HarperCollins Publishers.

"Roots," Reprinted with the permission of Beach Lane Books, an imprint of Simon & Schuster Children's Publishing Division from *Poetress* by Douglas Florian. Copyright © 2010 Douglas Florian.

"Summer full moon," Reprinted by permission of the James Kirkup Collection

"The moon is a white cat," from *The Sun is a Golden Earring* by Natalia Belting. Copyright © 1990 Natalia Belting. Reprinted by permission of Henry Holt & Company.

Sleuth

From: The Super Sleuths

Subject: Mysteries

Dear Sleuthhound,

A sleuth is a mystery solver. Mysteries are everywhere. There are everyday mysteries that happen in ordinary places. There are mysteries that take place far away in a land that you have never visited. This book is full of mysteries! We need a sleuthhound like you to look for clues. As a sleuth, it's important for you to ask interesting questions. Put all the clues and evidence together. Use the evidence to prove your answers! These Super Sleuth Steps will help you find answers to some great mysteries!

We're counting on you!

SUPER SLEUTH STEPS

Gather Evidence

- Look back at the pictures and reread the text. What do the clues tell you?
- Record the evidence. Write or draw what you find.
- Organize the important ideas. Try to put the clues together.

Ask Questions

- Great questions can be the key to solving a mystery.
- A sleuth is always curious.
- Keep asking questions. Questions can help you learn something amazing.

Make Your Case

- Look at all the clues. What conclusion can you make?
- State your position clearly. Be ready to convince others.
- Give good reasons to explain your thinking.

Prove It!

- Show what you have learned. This is your chance to shine!
- You may be working with others. Be certain that everyone has a chance to share the work and the fun!

Unit 1

Observing the World Around Us

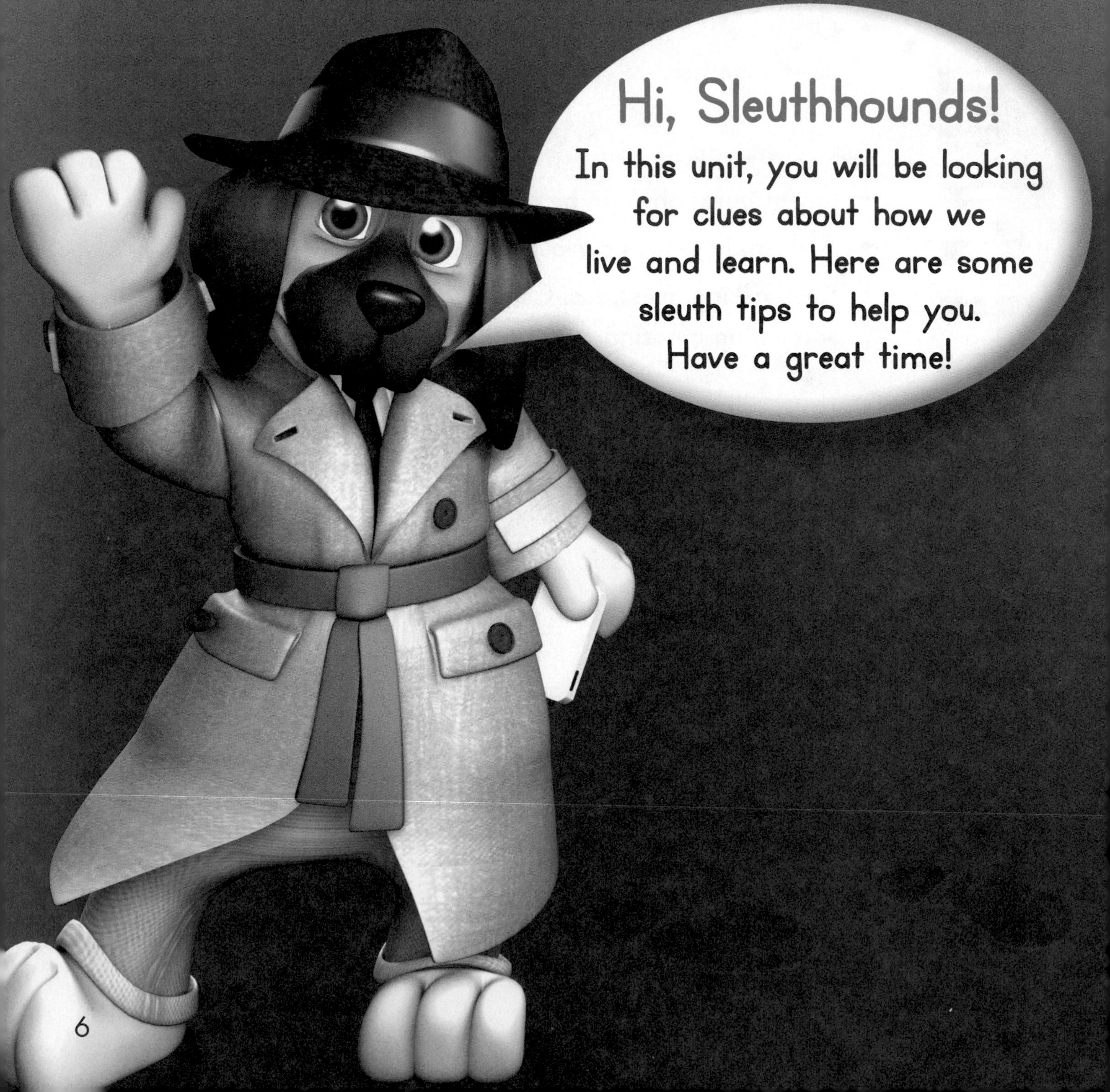

Sleuth Tips

Gather Evidence

Where do sleuths find clues?

- Sleuths look for clues as they read. Sometimes clues are easy to find, but other times they are hidden.
- Sleuths look for clues in the pictures. Not all clues are written in the text.

Ask Questions

What kinds of questions do sleuths ask?

- Sleuths ask many interesting and important questions to find clues!
- Sleuths ask when, where, why, and how something happened.

Make Your Case

How do sleuths decide on an answer?

- Sleuths look back and reread. Then they think about what they already know.
- Sleuths put the clues together. Clues help them decide on the best answer.

Prove It!

What do sleuths do to prove what they know?

- Sleuths think about all they have learned and decide which clues are important to share with others.
- Sleuths plan what they will write, draw, or explain. Sleuths check their work to make sure it is clear.

Getting ORGANIZED

Mrs. Rodriguez asked her students to turn in their homework. Cora's stomach sank because she didn't have her homework. She remembered to do it, but she forgot to put it in her backpack. It was still sitting on the kitchen table.

"Cora," Mrs. Rodriguez said, "did you forget to do your homework again?"

"No," Cora looked down at her feet. "I did the homework, but I left it at home."

"I'm sorry to hear that, Cora," Mrs. Rodriguez said. "Bring it in tomorrow, but you will lose five points."

That night the phone rang. "Hello, Mrs. Rodriguez," Cora heard her mother answer. *This cannot be good,* Cora thought.

"Of course, I will talk to Cora."

"Cora," Mama said, "Mrs. Rodriguez says your missing and late assignments are going to affect your grade. That's a problem."

"I'm sorry," Cora said. "I'm always in such a rush in the morning. It's hard to remember everything."

"Cora, rather than being sorry," Mama said, "I want you to solve this problem. You're too smart to let a lack of organization get in the way of good grades."

"What can I do, Mama?" Cora asked.

"Let's think of some ways you can be more organized," Mama said.

Cora came up with three solutions to her problem:

1. Write down my assignments.
2. Get ready for school the night before.
3. Have Mama double-check my homework.

Three weeks later, Cora brought home her report card. Mama gave her a hug. Cora's solutions had worked!

Sleuth Work

Gather Evidence Cora has been disorganized for a while. Write two details from the story that let you know about this problem.

Ask Questions What questions might the teacher have asked Cora to help understand why Cora's homework wasn't turned in on time? Write two questions.

Make Your Case How do you think Cora's decision to change her habits changes what happens in the rest of story?

Lin's Lesson

"You know you're not supposed to bring food downstairs," Mom said to Lin. She was walking up the stairs from Lin's bedroom holding a plate of dried-up sandwich. "When you leave food out, bugs come, and I can't stand bugs. If you want a snack, eat it upstairs."

"Yes, Mom," Lin said, only half paying attention. He didn't see what the big deal was and why she was so worried about bugs. The few he'd seen in his room were harmless little ants. Sometimes when he was drawing, he got so preoccupied that he forgot about the snacks he had brought downstairs.

The next morning, Lin woke up to a strange sensation. He opened his eyes and saw ants crawling over his arm. Lin bolted out of bed. Ants were crawling on the floor and in and out of the pretzel bag that was open on his desk. Lin ran upstairs, where he found his mom drinking her morning cup of tea.

"Mom!" Lin howled. "There are ants all over my room, even in my bed! I never thought this would happen!"

"Oh, Lin," Mom replied, "that's why we have rules—to avoid just this kind of thing. I'll have to call the exterminator, and you'll have to save your allowance and pay me back. Got it?"

"Yes, Mom. I'm really sorry." Lin had learned his lesson the hard way! He would have to use his own money to pay to get the ants removed.

Sleuth Work

Gather Evidence Choose either Lin or his mother. What details does the writer include to show how the person felt?

Ask Questions Write three questions you think Lin and his mom would ask each other about this experience a week after it happened.

Make Your Case Do you think Lin learned a lesson? Write three details from the text that support your answer.

A Whale of a Rescue

Imagine walking along the beach and stopping now and then to pick up an interesting shell. You see something at the water's edge. You realize it's a whale—a whale stranded on the beach.

Some animals, such as seals, often come out of the water onto the shore. But for whales, dolphins, and porpoises, this behavior usually means that something is wrong. Sometimes the animal is sick, but sometimes it has just lost its way. Swimming in stormy seas can exhaust some animals. Their exhaustion will make them disoriented. Others get stuck in shallow waters when the tide is outgoing.

One time, in February 2011, not just one whale, but 82 were stranded! For reasons unknown, 82 pilot whales became stranded on a beach in New Zealand.

The Department of Conservation of New Zealand, along with over 100 volunteers, came to the rescue. They worked all weekend long to get the animals back into the water. All but 17 whales made it.

Then, just days later, 65 whales were stranded again! This time, the volunteers didn't try to move the whales back into the water. "New evidence suggests that moving stranded whales causes them a lot of stress and pain," Department of Conservation ranger Simon Walls told a local newspaper. Instead, the volunteers cared for the whales on shore while waiting for the high tides to return.

All 65 of the newly stranded whales were successfully returned to the water. The plan had worked!

Sleuth Work

Gather Evidence What evidence can you find in the text to explain why whales might become stranded on the beach?

Ask Questions After reading the text, write three questions about the stranded pilot whales and the people who tried to help them.

Make Your Case What words does the author use to compare and contrast the two events? Do you think the events are more alike or more different?

BACKYARD SAFARI

Because I live in the city, I rarely see animals that I read about in school. When Dad takes me to the park, I see pigeons and squirrels. Boring! I want to see snakes and rabbits.

Last weekend I stayed with Aunt Marie in the country. Instead of going to the park, I played in Aunt Marie's backyard.

When we arrived at Aunt Marie's, I found her fixing breakfast and wearing a strange hat. "What's that on your head?" I asked.

"It's my safari hat!" She held up a smaller one and tossed it to me. Aunt Marie explained that we were going on a backyard safari.

I inhaled my breakfast. Then we set out toward the yard with binoculars and a magnifying glass.

"Do you hear that?" Aunt Marie asked.

I heard what sounded like a tiny jackhammer. She handed me the binoculars and told me to look high up in the tree. I soon found the source of the noise. It was a woodpecker with a red head.

Aunt Marie said that rabbits love to rest under her rose bushes. We lay in the grass and waited. As we waited, she told me all about the critters that call her backyard home—opossum, raccoons, chipmunks, and snakes. Some like to come out early in the morning, others at night.

Then something caught my eye. It was a ball of fur with a nose that was wiggling. "A rabbit," I whispered, even though I wanted to yell. Who knew I could see so much wildlife on a backyard safari!

SLEUTH WORK

Gather Evidence Write two clues that show the narrator was excited about the backyard safari.

Ask Questions After reading the text, write two questions you would ask an expert about animals that live near humans.

Make Your Case Use words from the text to compare and contrast where the narrator lived and where his aunt lived.

15

Acknowledgments

Photographs

Every effort has been made to secure permission and provide appropriate credit for photographic material. The publisher deeply regrets any omission and pledges to correct errors called to its attention in subsequent editions.

Unless otherwise acknowledged, all photographs are the property of Pearson Education, Inc.

Photo locators denoted as follows: Top (T), Center (C), Bottom (B), Left (L), Right (R), Background (Bkgd)

Cover Chandler Digital Art

4 (Bkgd) Nightman1965/Fotolia, (TL) PaulPaladin/Fotolia, (TR) kontur-vid/Fotolia, (C) Kev Llewellyn/Shutterstock, (BR) Zedcor Wholly Owned/Thinkstock; **5** (CR) Warakorn/Fotolia, (TR) rrrob/Fotolia, (BR) Hemera Technologies/Thinkstock; **8** (B)Brad Pict/Fotolia,(T) Carlos Caetano/Shutterstock, (TR) Rob/Fotolia; **9** (B) Michael Flippo/Fotolia, (C) Stockbyte/Thinkstock, (R) rrrob/Fotolia; **10** (T) Judex/Fotolia, (TL) Hemera Technologies/Thinkstock, (L) Brand X Pictures/Thinkstock; **10** (Bkgd) tuja66/Fotolia, (R) Tupungato/Fotolia; **11** (CR) Photos/Thinkstock, (BR) Les Cunliffe/Fotolia, (B) Jim Barber/Fotolia; **12** (T) lunamarina/Fotolia, (BR) Skyline/Fotolia, (Bkgd) Tim Cuff/Alamy; **13** Tersina Shieh/Fotolia; **14** (BL) Vilmos Varga/Fotolia, (CR) Hemera Technologies/Thinkstock, (B) Nat Ulrich/Fotolia; **15** (TL) Alfrendo Nature/Thinkstock, (CL) Tony Campbell/Fotolia, (R) Nikolai Sorokin/Fotolia; **15** (B) Paul Hill/Fotolia; **18** (TR) Tinnakorn Nukul/Fotolia, (Bkgd) xiaoloangge/Fotolia, (BL) canakris/Fotolia; **19** (B) Jens Ottoson/Fotolia, (TR) uckyo/Fotolia; **20** (Bkgd) paylessimages/Fotolia, (BL) joanna wnuk/Fotolia, **20** (CL) paylessimages/Fotolia; **20** (T) Shutterstock; **21** (TR) Etien/Fotolia,(CR) japolia/Fotolia; **22** (BL) rgbspace/Fotolia, (Bkgd) kenzo/Fotolia; **23** (TR) Craig Jewell/Fotolia,(BR) dzain/Fotolia; **24** (Bkgd) Maria Skaldina/Fotolia, (C) Philip Game/Alamy; **28** (L) Frank Anusewicz/Shutterstock; (Bkgd) Rossler/Fotolia; **29** Dudarev Mikhail/Shutterstock; **30** Zastol'skiy Victor Leonidovich/Shutterstock; **31** Shutterstock; **32** (Bkgd) panthesja/Fotolia, (TL) Veniamin Kraskov/Fotolia, (CR) NASA; **33** (T) Henryk Sadura/Fotolia, (TR) flame&star/Fotolia, (BC) Ilene MacDonald/Alamy; **33** (BL) NASA; **34** (T) tm-photo/Fotolia, (Bkgd) clearviewstock/Fotolia, (C) Link Art/Fotolia, (TC) Anton Prado Photo/Fotolia; **34** (BC) MOKreations/Fotolia, (T) chas; **53**/Fotolia, (C) Comstock/Thinkstock; **35** (TR) Nikolai Sorokin/Foto, (B) andesign101/Fotolia; **38** (BL) Everett Collection Inc/Alamy, (TR) Steve Petteway/Supreme Court of the United States; **39** (TR) Library of Congress,(BR) Library of Congress; **40** (Bkgd) Galyna Andrushko/Fotolia, (B) Douglas Graham/Newscom; **41** (TR) National Archives,(CR) Tech Sgt.Craig Clapper/United States Air Force.

Reader's and Writer's Journal

Name _____

1. What did you read?
2. What did you learn?
3. What questions do you have?

Lesson 1

1. _____

2. _____

3. _____

Lesson 2

1. _____

2. _____

3. _____

Lesson 3

1. _____

2. _____

3. _____

Lesson 4

1. _____

2. _____

3. _____

Lesson 5

1. _____

2. _____

3. _____

Name _____

Getting Organized

Mrs. Rodriguez asked her students to turn in their homework. Cora's stomach sank because she didn't have her homework. She remembered to do it, but she forgot to put it in her backpack. It was still sitting on the kitchen table.

"Cora," Mrs. Rodriguez said, "did you forget to do your homework again?"

"No," Cora looked down at her feet. "I did the homework, but I left it at home."

"I'm sorry to hear that, Cora," Mrs. Rodriguez said. "Bring it in tomorrow, but you will lose five points."

That night the phone rang. "Hello, Mrs. Rodriguez," Cora heard her mother answer. *This cannot be good,* Cora thought.

"Of course, I will talk to Cora."

"Cora" Mama said, "Mrs. Rodriguez says your missing and late assignments are going to affect your grade. That's a problem."

"I'm sorry," Cora said. "I'm always in such a rush in the morning. It's hard to remember everything."

"Cora, rather than being sorry," Mama said, "I want you to solve this problem. You're too smart to let a lack of organization get in the way of good grades."

"What can I do, Mama?" Cora asked.

"Let's think of some ways you can be more organized," Mama said.

Cora came up with three solutions to her problem:

1. Write down my assignments.

2. Get ready for school the night before.

3. Have Mama double-check my homework.

Three weeks later, Cora brought home her report card. Mama gave her a hug. Cora's solutions had worked!

Gather Evidence On page 2, circle 3–4 details about Cora's problem that are in the text. In another color, box which 2 are most important to the story. Write those two details below.

Gather Evidence: Extend Your Ideas Work with a partner and discuss how changing just one of these details would affect the story.

Ask Questions Write two questions that the teacher might have asked Cora about why Cora's homework wasn't turned in on time. Underline the words in the text that could answer the questions.

Ask Questions: Extend Your Ideas Write an additional question that the teacher could have asked Cora that is answered in the text. Underline the answer in the text.

Make Your Case Draw an arrow *from* Cora's decision (a cause) about changing her habits *to* what happens (the effect) at the end of the story.

Make Your Case: Extend Your Ideas Identify other causes that lead to other effects. Discuss your results with a partner.

Lesson 1

earned _____

_____

equation _____

_____

Lesson 2

gimmick _____

_____

competition _____

_____

Lesson 3

frozen air _____

_____

no-smiling, I'm-not-your-buddy mask _____

_____

Lesson 4

laboratory _____

_____

solution _____

_____

Lesson 5

observations _____

_____

mediums _____

_____

Name _____

Lesson 1 Reread page 26 from the Text Set Collection. Write several sentences that describe Evan's actions, motivations, and feelings.

Lesson 2 Reread the last paragraph on page 32 and the first on page 33 from the Text Set Collection. Write a paragraph that explains the sequence of events in the two paragraphs that you reread. Include words and phrases that show the order of events.

Lesson 3 Reread pages 25–39 from the Text Set Collection. What is your opinion of Evan's solution to his problem? State your opinion and support it using evidence from the text.

Lesson 4 Reread page 3 of *The Case of the Gasping Garbage*. Write a short narrative from Gabby's point of view that tells what happens before she calls Doyle and asks for his help. Use evidence from the text to establish the details and events.

Lesson 5 Lesson 5 Reread pp. 13–15 of *The Case of the Gasping Garbage*. Using evidence from the text, write an explanation of the procedure (steps) that Drake and Nell use to solve the garbage can problem.

Using evidence from the text, answer the following questions about Chapters 1 and 2 from *The Case of the Gasping Garbage*.

1. Who are the characters in Chapter 1? Who are the characters in Chapter 2?

   _____

   _____

   _____

2. Why are some characters the same in the two chapters? Why are some characters different?

   _____

   _____

3. What settings are the same in both chapters?

   _____

4. What are the most important events in Chapter 1? Why are they important?

   _____

   _____

   _____

5. What are the most important events in Chapter 2? Why are they important?

   _____

   _____

   _____

1. Reread the first two complete paragraphs on page 31 of "Location, Location, Location."

2. What key words and phrases does the author use to show the sequence of the events?

   _____

3. Explain how these words help you understand the sequence of events.

   _____

   _____

   _____

4. Reread the sentences on page 36 of "Location, Location, Location." Notice how the author is using the word *then*. How does the author's use of the word *then* change what happens?

   _____

   _____

5. Explain how the use of the word *then* is different in the two sections that you reread.

   _____

   _____

   _____

Name _____

Lesson 1 Nouns Circle the nouns in the sentences.
1. Evan dragged his wagon to the center of the town.

2. Evan went to his desk and worked on some problems.

Lesson 2 Form Regular Plural Nouns Write the plural of each word.

1. buzz _____   2. dollar _____   3. church _____

4. minus _____   5. eyelash _____   6. fax _____

Lesson 3 Use Regular Nouns Write an sentence using one of the following nouns: bough, kids, Evan, center.

_____

Lesson 4 Identify Verbs Reread page 3 of The Case of the Gasping Garbage. Find four words that are verbs and write them.

_____   _____

_____   _____

Lesson 5 Form Regular Verbs Write the verb.

Verb	Present Tense		Past Tense	Present Participle
to earn	no ending	add ending: -s	add ending: -ed	add ending: -ing
	earn	earns	earned	Earning
	I _____	*He* _____.	*They* _____.	*You are* _____.

Lesson 1 Write a narrative paragraph using full sentences that form a paragraph.

_____

_____

_____

_____

_____

Lesson 2 Use Dialogue to Show Character Reaction Write a narrative paragraph with realistic events and characters.

_____

_____

_____

_____

_____

Lesson 3 Write a Narrative On a separate piece of paper, write a paragraph of realistic fictional narrative with a realistic setting.

Lesson 4 Write a Narrative Write a fictional narrative paragraph that introduces a character, an interesting setting, and the event that starts the story. Make sure to use these elements to establish a situation.

_____

_____

_____

_____

_____

Lesson 5 Write a fictional narrative paragraph that continues the narrative you wrote in Lesson 4. Make sure to continue the situation from the first paragraph, resolve the situation, and establish a new situation.

_____

_____

_____

_____

_____

Name _____

1. What did you read?
2. What did you learn?
3. What questions do you have?

Lesson 6

1. _____

2. _____

3. _____

Lesson 7

1. _____

2. _____

3. _____

Lesson 8

1. _____

2. _____

3. _____

Lesson 9

1. _____

2. _____

3. _____

Lesson 10

1. _____

2. _____

3. _____

Using evidence from the text, answer the following questions about *The Case of the Gasping Garbage*.

1. Reread the first sentence in the last paragraph on p. 39. What word in the sentence is used in a nonliteral way?

   _____

2. What is the literal meaning of the word *heart*?

   _____

3. What is the nonliteral meaning of the word as it is used in the book?

   _____

4. Write a new sentence using the word hurt in a nonliteral way.

   _____

   _____

Using evidence from the text, answer the following questions about
The Case of the Gasping Garbage.

1. Reread p. 24 and 25 in *The Case of the Gasping Garbage*. Describe how chapter 3 ends.

   _____

   _____

2. Describe how chapter 4 begins.

3. What does Chapter 4 develop, or build on, from chapter 3?

   _____

   _____

4. Why does the author do this?

   _____

   _____

   _____

Name _____

Lesson 6

graph _____

_____

aquariums _____

_____

Lesson 7

global warming _____

_____

pollution _____

_____

Lesson 8

dark day _____

_____

archrival _____

_____

Lesson 9

air pressure _____

_____

valve _____

_____

Lesson 10

hypothesis _____

_____

evidence _____

_____

Lesson 6 Reread the fourth paragraph on p. 20 of *The Case of the Gasping Garbage*. The narrator makes statements about Nell Fossey. Does your own reading fit this analysis? State your opinion and support it using text evidence.

Lesson 7 How would you describe Doyle and Fossey's motivations and actions? What do they do to show motivation? Use an example from the text to support your answer.

Lesson 8 Reread the paragraph on p. 32 of *The Case of the Gasping Garbage* that begins "This is a chance for Doyle and Fossey." Write a brief narrative in which you retell this part of the story from Frisco's perspective.

Lesson 9 Reread the third paragraph on p. 43 of *The Case of the Gasping Garbage*. The narrator states Fossey's tadpoles were glad to see her. Describe Fossey's experience when she finally got home.

Lesson 10 Reread p. 50 of *The Case of the Gasping Garbage*. How might you have gone about your investigation differently than Doyle and Fossey went about their investigation? State your opinion and support it using text evidence.

Using evidence from the text, answer the following questions about
Chapter 5 from *The Case of the Gasping Garbage*.

1. What is the sequence of events?

_____

_____

_____

2. What does Fossey do to contribute to these events? What does Doyle
do to contribute to these events?

_____

_____

_____

3. Compare and contrast the impact of Fossey's and Doyle's actions on
the sequence of events.

_____

_____

_____

4. What are the most important events in Chapter 5? Why are they
important?

_____

_____

_____

1. Reread p. 18 in Chapter 3 of *The Case of the Gasping Garbage*. What key words and phrases does the author use to show the order in which events happen?

_____

2. Explain how these words help you understand the sequence of events.

_____

_____

_____

3. Reread the sentences on p. 18 in Chapter 3 of *The Case of the Gasping Garbage*. Notice how the author using the word *after*. What happens *after* school on Friday?

_____

_____

4. Explain how the use of the word *after* helps you understand the sequence of events.

_____

_____

Lesson 6 Form Simple Sentences Using Regular Verbs Write a sentence using at least one noun and one verb. Circle the verb you use.

1. Doyle washed the dishes and the beaker in the lab.

2. Today, the newspaper reporters called them heroes.

Lesson 7 Irregular Plural Nouns Write the plural of each word.
1. buzz _____   2. tax _____   3. lunch _____
4. minus _____   5. splash _____   6. echo _____

Lesson 8 How Nouns Function in a Sentence Circle the subject in the following sentences:
Doyle couldn't believe it was them.

He wanted to find a way for the frogs to cross the street safely.

Fossey found the answer and wrote it down in her book.

She said that she could not remember.

Lesson 9 Identify Irregular Verbs that End in -y Write a sentence using at least one of the following verbs in past tense: scurry, bury, hurry. Circle the verb in your sentence.

Lesson 10 Identify the Function of Verbs Read the sentences below. Circle the verbs in each sentence.
Knowing this, Nell picked up a strong twig
and calmly poked it into the valve of tire number one.
She stared at the tires.
And then she knew. It was simple.

_____

Name _____

Lesson 6 Introduce a Character Continuing with the narrative you began in Lesson and continued in Lesson 5, write a series of events that are organized into a logical sequence.

_____

_____

_____

_____

Lesson 7 Use Dialogue to Show Character Reaction Write a character sketch of Nell Fossey, tracking Nell's character traits, motivations, and feelings and using information they collected.

_____

_____

_____

_____

_____

Lesson 8 Write a Narrative On a separate piece of paper, write a narrative of dialogue that reveals a character's response using a character or two from their narrative in Lessons 4-6 and crafting the dialogue so that it reveals a character response.

Lesson 9 Write a Narrative Write a narrative that uses description of actions, thoughts, and feelings to character experiences. Make sure to use and/or continue the narrative they began in Lesson 4 and use descriptive details of actions, thoughts, and feelings to develop the character's experiences.

_____

_____

_____

_____

Lesson 10 Write a Narrative Write a narrative using descriptions of actions, thoughts, and feelings to describe a character's thoughts. Make sure to continue the narrative you began in Lesson 4, record traits, motivations, and feelings of the character by carefully examining his or her speech, actions, and/or thoughts, and use the collected information to draft character responses.

_____

_____

_____

_____

1. What did you read?
2. What did you learn?
3. What questions do you have?

Lesson 11

1. _____

2. _____

3. _____

Lesson 12

1. _____

2. _____

3. _____

Lesson 13

1. _____

2. _____

3. _____

Lesson 14

1. _____

2. _____

3. _____

Lesson 15

1. _____

2. _____

3. _____

Lin's Lesson

"You know you're not supposed to bring food downstairs," Mom said to Lin. She was walking up the stairs from Lin's bedroom holding a plate of dried-up sandwich. "When you leave food out, bugs come, and I can't stand bugs. If you want a snack, eat it upstairs."

"Yes, Mom," Lin said, only half paying attention. He didn't see what the big deal was and why she was so worried about bugs. The few he'd seen in his room were harmless little ants. Sometimes when he was drawing, he got so preoccupied that he forgot about the snacks he had brought downstairs.

The next morning, Lin woke up to a strange sensation. He opened his eyes and saw ants crawling over his arm. Lin bolted out of bed. Ants were crawling on the floor and in and out of the pretzel bag that was open on his desk. Lin ran upstairs, where he found his mom drinking her morning cup of tea.

"Mom!" Lin howled. "There are ants all over my room, even in my bed! I never thought this would happen!"

"Oh, Lind," Mom replied, "that's why we have rules—to avoid just this kind of thing. I'll have to call the exterminator, and you'll have to save your allowance and pay me back. Got it?"

"Yes, Mom. I'm really sorry." Lin had learned his lesson the hard way! He would have to use his own money to pay to get the ants removed.

Gather Evidence Circle 3 details from "Lin's Lesson" to support whether or not Lin learns his lesson. In another color, circle which detail best supports whether Lin learns his lesson. Write the detail below.

_____

Gather Evidence: Extend Your Ideas Briefly explain why the circled details are important to the story. Then work with a partner and discuss how changing just one of these details would affect the story.

_____

Ask Questions Write two questions you think Lin and his mom would ask each other about this experience a week after it happened. Underline any words that could help answer the first question. Underline twice any words that could help answer the second question.

_____

_____

Ask Questions: Extend Your Ideas Did you underline any words in the text that would answer your questions? If the answer is yes, explain. If the answer is no, write an additional question that is answered in the text, and include that answer with your new question.

_____

_____

Make Your Case Choose either Lin or his mother. Circle 3–4 details the writer includes to show how the character feels.

Make Your Case: Extend Your Ideas Why is it so important to express how characters are feeling in a story? Write a sentence or two explaining how essential Lin's or his mother's feelings are to the story. How would the story be different if the feelings were exchanged?

_____

_____

Name _____

Lesson 11

slid _____

_____

dreadful _____

_____

Lesson 12

intelligent _____

_____

motivation _____

_____

Lesson 13

dry shed _____

_____

trellis _____

_____

Lesson 14

surveyed _____

_____

squinted _____

_____

Lesson 15

horizon _____

_____

sultry _____

_____

Name _____

Lesson 11 Skim through chapter 8 of *The Case of the Gasping Garbage* to remind yourself of its main points. Now that the author of the love letter has been revealed, write a mysterious narrative of your own. Keep in mind that characters' actions impact the sequence of events in a story.

Lesson 12 Reread p. 16–17 in *The Case of the Gasping Garbage* and p. 98–100 in *The Lemonade War*. Write an essay comparing and contrasting the way Doyle and Fosscy and Evan identify problems and find solutions. Support your answers using text evidence.

Lesson 13 Reread p. 12 of *Thunder Cake*. The narrator says she was scared while walking to Tanglewced Woods to collect the ingredients from the dry shed. Why do you think she was scared? State your opinion and support it using text evidence.

Lesson 14 Reread p. 5 of *Thunder Cake*. This introduction is told from the granddaughter's point of view. Retell the introduction to *Thunder Cake* from Grandma's point of view.

Lesson 15 15 Reread pp. 5–8 of *Thunder Cake*. Write a paragraph or two explaining why Grandma chose to bake a Thunder Cake. Use text evidence to support your explanation.

Using evidence from the text, answer the following questions about *The Case of the Gasping Garbage.*

1. How does the narrator describe her fear of thunder?

_____

_____

2. How does she initially respond to it?

_____

_____

3. How do you think the narrator feels when her grandmother asks for her help gathering the ingredients for Thunder Cake?

_____

_____

4. How do her feelings differ from her response?

_____

_____

5. How does the very last page of the story build on the very first page of the story?

_____

_____

_____

Name _____

1. Reread p. 5 of *Thunder Cake* in the text collection. What are some descriptive words the author uses to describe characters or setting?

_____

_____

2. Explain how the author uses these descriptive details to develop the setting.

_____

_____

_____

3. What effect does this have on the story?

_____

_____

_____

4. Reread the sentences on p. 14 of *Thunder Cake*. How does the author use descriptive details to develop grandma's character?

_____

_____

_____

5. What effect do these words and phrases have on the story?

_____

_____

_____

Lesson 11 Form Simple Sentences With Nouns, Temporal Words, and Verbs Write a sentence with one noun, one temporal word, and one verb.

Lesson 12 Identify Forms of Irregular Verbs Circle the verb in the sentence:

Doyle and Fossey hurried home.

Lesson 13 Form the Simple Verb Tenses Form the past, present and future tenses of each verb.

Past Tense	Present Tense	Future Tense
I walked.	*I walk.*	*I will walk.*
	He gathers.	
She invented.		
_____	_____	_____

Lesson 14 Form a Simple Sentence Using a Noun and an Irregular Verb Write a sentence using at least one noun and irregular verb ending in y.

Lesson 15 Identify Pronouns Underline the pronouns that are used as subjects, circle the pronouns that are direct objects, and put a check mark over he pronouns that are indirect objects.

Doyle couldn't believe it was them.

He wanted to find a way for the frogs to cross the street safely.

Fossey found the answer and wrote it down in her book.

She said that she could not remember.

Lesson 11 Introduce a Character write a one-paragraph narrative that clearly illustrates your understanding of how temporal words and phrases are used to signal event order and organize an event sequence.

_____

_____

_____

_____

_____

Lesson 12 Use Dialogue to Show Character Reaction Write a narrative that introduces a problem in the beginning and provides a sense of closure.

_____

_____

_____

_____

_____

Lesson 13 Write a Narrative Write a brief narrative that provides a sense of closure and continues the narrative you began in Lesson 4.

_____

_____

_____

_____

_____

_____

_____

_____

Lesson 14 Write a Narrative Write a story similar to *Thunder Cake* in which you write about a time where a problem was solved by using your best thinking.

Lesson 15 How the Author Reveals Information Revise the story you started in lesson 14, using dialogue to show the response of the characters to the events. Make sure to revise the sequence of events so that it unfolds naturally.

_____

_____

_____

_____

Name _____

1. What did you read?
2. What did you learn?
3. What questions do you have?

Lesson 16

1. _____

2. _____

3. _____

Lesson 17

1. _____

2. _____

3. _____

Lesson 18

1. _____

2. _____

3. _____

Using evidence from the text, answer the following questions about "Location, Location, Location" and *Thunder Cake*.

1. Describe how Evan identifies problems and finds solutions.

_____

_____

_____

2. Describe how Grandma identifies problems and finds solutions.

_____

_____

_____

3. How is Evan's process for identifying problems and finding solutions different than Grandma's

_____

_____

_____

4. How is it similar?

_____

_____

_____

Lesson 16

experiment _____

_____

flask _____

_____

Lesson 17

convince _____

_____

scorcher _____

_____

Lesson 18

luscious _____

_____

scurried _____

_____

Lesson 16 Reread p. 18 in *The Case of the Gasping Garbage* from "It was Friday after school..." to "Mrs. Doyle closed the door." Then reread p. 7 in *Thunder Cake* from "'Steady child...'" to "'Thunder Cake' I stammered as I hugged her even closer." Which text do you think uses narrative techniques most effectively? State your opinion and then support your opinion with reasons and evidence from the text.

Lesson 17 Reread p. 31 from "He needed a plan" to "He just needed to find something with wheels to get him there" in *Location, Location, Location*. Then reread p. 18 from "The air was hot, heavy and damp" to "'Thunder Cake?' I stammered as I hugged her even closer." Write an essay comparing and contrasting the way Grandma and Evan identify problems and find solutions. Support your answers using text evidence.

Lesson 18 Reread p. 18 in *The Case of the Gasping Garbage* from "It was Friday after school..." to "Mrs. Doyle closed the door." Then reread p. 20 in *Thunder Cake* from "But you got out from under it" to "'From where I sit, only a very brave person could have done all them things!'" Finally, reread p. 30 in *The Lemonade War* from "It took Evan half an hour to drag his loaded wagon to the town center" to "But once he was there, he knew it was worth it." Compare and contrast the way in which one character from each text changes over time. Support your answers using text evidence.

Name _____

Focus on p. 18 of *The Case of the Gasping Garbage* and p. 7 in *Thunder Cake*

1. What narrative techniques are found in *The Case of the Gasping Garbage*?

_____

_____

2. Which details in *The case of the Gasping Garbage* demonstrate the narrative techniques used by the author?

_____

_____

3. What narrative techniques are found in *Thunder Cake*?

_____

_____

_____

4. Which details in *Thunder Cake* demonstrate the narrative techniques used by the author?

_____

_____

_____

Name _____

Using evidence from the text, answer the following questions about *The Case of the Gasping Garbage, Thunder Cake* and "Location, Location, Location"

1. Focus on p. 18 of *The Case of the Gasping Garbage*, p. 18 in *Thunder Cake*, and p. 31 in "Location, Location, Location." How do Doyle and Fossey contribute to the sequence of events?

   _____

   _____

   _____

2. How does the narrator in *Thunder Cake* contribute to the sequence of events?

   _____

   _____

   _____

3. How does Evan contribute to the sequence of events?

   _____

   _____

4. How does the contributions of each character in each of these stories differ? How are they the same?

   _____

   _____

Lesson 16 Use Pronouns Read the passage below. Circle the nouns and replace them with pronouns.

Fossey and Doyle can solve a problem by using their smarts, working in the lab, or talking with friends.

Lesson 17 Use Commas in Dialogue Insert commas into the dialogue where appropriate.

1. "I am tired " Evan said.
2. The detective thought "I can solve anything!"

Lesson 18 Use Quotation Marks in Dialogue Use quotation marks to separate dialogue from description.

1. Where did you find that frog?   asked Joe.
2. Mother said   I want you to come home for dinner.
3. Where is my hat?   wailed the toddler.

Name _____

Lesson 16 Introduce a Character Continuing your narrative from Lesson 14, revise your narrative so that a problem is clearly presented at the beginning and solved by the end.

_____

_____

_____

_____

_____

Lesson 17 Use Dialogue to Show Character Reaction Edit the story you began in Lesson 4. Like "Thunder Cake," the story should begin with a clear problem and be solved by the end. Use material based on your own experiences of a time where fear turned into courage or a problem was solved by using your best thinking.

_____

_____

_____

_____

Lesson 18 Write a Narrative Publish and present your narratives. Make sure to read your narrative to the class and publish your narratives on a blog.

_____

_____

_____

_____

_____

1. What did you read?
2. What did you learn?
3. What questions do you have?

Lesson 1

1. _____
2. _____
3. _____

Lesson 2

1. _____
2. _____
3. _____

Lesson 3

1. _____
2. _____
3. _____

Lesson 4

1. _____
2. _____
3. _____

Lesson 5

1. _____
2. _____
3. _____

A Whale of a Rescue

Imagine walking along the beach and stopping now and then to pick up an interesting shell. You see something at the water's edge. You realize it's a whale—a whale stranded on the beach.

Some animals, such as seals, often come out of the water onto the shore. But for whales, dolphins and porpoises, this behavior usually means that something is wrong. Sometimes the animal is sick, but sometimes it has just lost its way. Swimming in stormy seas can exhaust some animals. Their exhaustion will make them disoriented. Others get stuck in shallow waters when the tide is outgoing.

One time, in February 2011, not just one whale, but 82 were stranded! For reasons unknown, 82 pilot whales became stranded on a beach in New Zealand.

The Department of Conservation of New Zealand, along with over 100 volunteers, came to the rescue. They worked all weekend long to get the animals back into the water. All but 17 whales made it.

Then, just days later, 65 whales were stranded again! This time, the volunteers didn't try to move the whales back into the water. "New evidence suggests that moving stranded whales causes them a lot of stress and pain," Department of Conservation ranger Simon Walls told a local newspaper. Instead, the volunteers cared for the whales on shore while waiting for the high tides to return.

All 65 of the newly-stranded whales were successfully returned to the water. The plan had worked!

Gather Evidence Highlight 3–4 pieces of evidence from A Whale of a Rescue to explain why whales might become stranded on the beach.

_____

_____

_____

Gather Evidence: Extend Your Ideas Work with a partner and discuss how changing just one of these details would affect the story.

_____

_____

Ask Questions Write three questions about the stranded pilot whales and the people who try to help them. Underline any text from A Whale of a Rescue that could help answer your first question. Underline twice any text that could help answer your second question. Draw a box around any text that could help answer your third question.

_____

_____

Ask Questions: Extend Your Ideas Did you underline any words from A Whale of a Rescue that would answer your questions? If the answer is yes, explain. If the answer is no, write an additional question about stranded pilot whales and the people who try to help them that is answered in the text, and include that answer with your new question.

_____

_____

Make Your Case What words does the author use to compare and contrast the two events in the selection? Draw a circle around the words from A Whale of a Rescue.

Make Your Case: Extend Your Ideas Write 2–3 sentences comparing and contrasting the two events.

Lesson 1
waxing _____

_____

waning _____

_____

Lesson 2
sliver _____

_____

crescent _____

_____

Lesson 3
phases _____

_____

Lesson 4
creep _____

_____

root _____

_____

Lesson 5
flexible _____

_____

minerals _____

_____

Name _____

Lesson 1 Reread p. 43 from "The Moon Seems to Change" and study the illustrations. According to the text, "the moon seems to change." As the nights pass and you can see changes in the moon, the moon itself seems to change. Does your own reading of "The Moon Seems To Change" support this? Try to observe the moon's phases yourself. State your opinion and support it using text evidence.

Lesson 2 Reread p. 55 from "The Moon Seems To Change" and have students write a paragraph explaining how the phases of the moon cause the moon to seem to change. Be sure students support their writing using text-based evidence.

Lesson 3 Reread p. 50 of "The Moon Seems To Change" Look at the illustration and write about what you see. What do you prefer about the waxing moon? State your opinion and support it using text evidence.

Lesson 4 Reread the paragraph on p. 11. Have students write a paragraph that explains how the different types of roots that plants have capture water. Remind students to support their writing using text evidence.

Lesson 5 Reread p. 6 of *At the Root of It*. Have students write an informative/explanatory paragraph about the importance of a plant's root system. Remind students to support their writing using text evidence.

Lesson 1

Using evidence from the text, answer the following questions about
text features.

1. Look at the diagram on page 46. What main idea should readers
   understand about a day on Earth compared to a day on the moon?

   _____

   _____

   _____

2. Look at the diagram on page 47. What is the main idea?

   _____

   _____

   _____

3. How does the diagram help readers understand why people see the
   moon at night?

   _____

   _____

   _____

4. Look at the diagram on page 55. What is the main idea?

   _____

   _____

   _____

5. State three facts or details about the diagram Phases of the Moon on
   page 55.

   _____

   _____

   _____

Lesson 2

1. Reread the first three sentences on page 45. Pay close attention to the word *same*. By using the word *same* is the writer making a comparison or a contrast?

   _____

   What does a comparison tell a reader?

   _____

2. What is the writer comparing in these sentences?

   _____

   _____

   _____

3. Reread the sentence on page 45 beginning with "While one half of Earth…" Which signal word does the writer use to show a comparison or contrast?

   _____

   _____

   _____

4. What two things are being contrasted in the sentence?

   _____

   _____

   _____

Lesson 1 Define Nouns as Subjects Circle the noun and subject in the sentence.

The moon seems to change.

Explain how the noun is used as a subject in this sentence.

Lesson 2 Use A Noun as A Subject Write the plural of each word.

Use a noun as a subject to complete the sentence from the text.

The _____ is waxing.

Lesson 3 Subject-Verb Agreement Past Tense

Identify the plural, past-tense form of is in a sentence:

(The cows _____ hungry.)

Lesson 4 Subject-Verb Agreement Past Tense

Complete the sentences from page 17.

One _____ in Darwin, Australia, destroyed almost every boat in the Darwin harbor.

Only two boats were _____.

What do you notice about the verb-spellings when combined with singular and plural subjects? Why?

Lesson 5 Produce Simple Sentences Using Subject-Verb Agreement Past Tense

Write a sentence in the past-tense. Explain how the verb agrees with the subject.

Lesson 1 Write a paragraph that uses facts and key details to explain a topic. Make sure to list three facts that develop and explain your topic.

_____

_____

_____

_____

_____

_____

_____

Lesson 2 Write an Expository Paragraph Choose one of the topics that you have brainstormed and write an outline that lists facts and details that you would include in scientific informational texts. Make sure to list facts and details about the topic in sentence form and expand on each fact with additional details.

_____

_____

_____

_____

_____

_____

_____

Lesson 3 Write a Topic Sentence On a separate piece of paper, using your explanatory text from Lessons 1 and 2, decide which fact or facts could be better expressed as an illustration and draw an illustration.

Lesson 4 Write a Paragraph Write one or two introductory sentences that introduces a topic. Decide what is the main idea of the text and write one or two sentences that describe the main idea.

_____

_____

_____

_____

Lesson 5 Write an Expository Text Building on the idea introduced in Lesson 4, identify important facts and key details, and use your Three-Column Chart to group together related information.

_____

_____

_____

_____

Name _____

1. What did you read?
2. What did you learn?
3. What questions do you have?

Lesson 6

1. _____

2. _____

3. _____

Lesson 7

1. _____

2. _____

3. _____

Lesson 8

1. _____

2. _____

3. _____

Lesson 9

1. _____

2. _____

3. _____

Lesson 10

1. _____

2. _____

3. _____

Lesson 8

Using evidence from the text, answer the following questions about main ideas.

1. Read the paragraph on page 20. What is the main idea?

   _____

   _____

2. Identify two key details that support the main idea.

   _____

   _____

3. Read the paragraph on page 20 titled *Is It a Root—or Not*? What is the main idea?

   _____

   _____

4. Reread pages 21–22. What is the main idea about roots?

   _____

   _____

5. Explain two ways roots are useful to animals.

   _____

   _____

6. Read the sentence on page 22 that begins "Roots are one of the. . ." Use at least two details from the text to support the main idea.

   _____

   _____

Lesson 7 pp. 14–19

1. On p. 15, find the word "nutrients." Explain two ways to use the word *nutrients* to tell about something in real-life.

   _____

   _____

   _____

   _____

2. What is one way you can use the word *nutrients* to tell about something in the world?

   _____

   _____

   _____

3. On p. 17, how does the word *sturdy* apply to your life?

   _____

   _____

   _____

4. What are some things in the world that could be described as *sturdy*? Explain.

   _____

   _____

   _____

Lesson 6

*absorb*_____

_____

taproot _____

_____

Lesson 7

hydroponics _____

_____

Lesson 8

bulb _____

_____

dens _____

_____

Lesson 9

sprouts _____

_____

tangled _____

_____

Lesson 10

tropical _____

_____

epiphytes _____

_____

Name _____

Lesson 6 Reread *At the Root of It* on p. 6. Have students write an opinion paragraph about which type of roots they think do a better job of capturing water--taproots or fibrous roots. Remind students to support their writing using text evidence.

Lesson 7 Reread the section of *At the Root of It* called "Roots Above Ground." Ask students to write a paragraph explaining how the author uses photos to explain the contrasts between types of roots and how this information allows readers to locate information efficiently. Remind students to use text evidence to support their answers.

Lesson 8 Reread *Root Facts,* pp. 20–22. Ask students to write a narrative about the importance of roots to all living things. Remind students to support their writing "using text evidence."

Lesson 9 Reread p. 3 and other pages from *At the Root of It* that feature literal and nonliteral expressions. Have students locate and describe examples of words or phrases that are literal and nonliteral. Have students support their examples by "using text evidence" from clues in the sentence or surrounding sentences.

Lesson 10 Reread *At the Root of It*. Then reread p. 22. The author states the opinion that roots may not be as pretty as flowers and leaves but they are still important. Write why you think roots are important to plants and to us. State your opinion and support it using text evidence.

Lesson 10

Using evidence from the text, answer the following questions about information from illustrations.

1. Look at the photo on p. 4. What does the photo help readers understand about trees?

   _____

   _____

2. Look at the model and photo on p. 8. What are root hairs?

   _____

   _____

3. Look at the model and photo on p. 8. How do the differences between the photo and the model help readers understand how roots absorb water?

   _____

   _____

4. Look at the pictures on p. 9. What does comparing the pictures tell readers about roots?

   _____

   _____

5. Read the text and look at the pictures on p. 10. What information should readers know about roots after looking at the pictures?.

   _____

   _____

Lesson 9

Using evidence from the text, answer the following questions about word relationships.

1. Read the first sentence on p. 3 that begins *"They creep…"* What is the literal meaning of the word "creep" in the sentence?

   _____

2. What is the author's purpose for using the word *creep* instead of a word with literal meaning?

   _____

   _____

3. Read the sentence on p. 5 that begins "Many roots look like…" What is the author comparing to roots?

   _____

4. Read the paragraph on p. 7 that begins "Roots are strong and flexible…" How does using non-literal words like *push through, break up, wind through, wrap around* instead of using literal words like *grow* or *grow around* make the writing stronger?

   _____

   _____

   _____

5. Read the sentence on p. 8 that begins *"It's the roots' job…"* Does the word "job" have the same meaning as a person's job in real life? Explain.

   _____

   _____

   _____

Lesson 6 Subject-Verb Agreement Present Tense

Reread page 13. Choose a sentence with a present tense verb and write it here. Explain how readers can tell the subject and verb in the sentence agree with each other.

_____

_____

Lesson 7 Produce Simple Sentences Using Subject-Verb Agreement Present Tense

Write a sentence in present tense with correct subject-verb agreement.

Lesson 8 Subject-Verb Agreement Future Tense

Fill in the blank to complete the sentence with the correct future tense verb.

John _____ a lap. (run)

Lesson 9 Produce Simple Sentences Using Subject-Verb Agreement Future Tense

Write a sentence in future tense with correct subject-verb agreement.

Lesson 10 Adjectives: Definition

Read this sentence from page 3: "They hold up the biggest trees and the smallest sprouts." What words could replace biggest or smallest in this sentence? Explain how the adjective is used in the sentence.

Lesson 6 Write an Introductory Paragraph Using your Three-Column Charts from Lesson 5, write several paragraphs expanding your ideas and using linking words and phrases to connect ideas. Make sure each paragraph is a category from the organizer.

_____

_____

_____

_____

_____

_____

_____

_____

Lesson 7 Write an Introductory Paragraph Compare and contrast two informational texts on the same topic, stating which text best explains the information, explaining why you believe that text best explains the information, and using linking words and phrases.

_____

_____

_____

_____

_____

_____

_____

_____

Lesson 8 Write an Expository Text Complete a Main Idea graphic organizer and list the facts, definitions, and details that will develop your topic and support the main idea.

_____

_____

_____

_____

_____

Lesson 9 Write a Paragraph Create a "Discovery Channel" science skit with informational visuals that can accompany your skit. Make sure to use fun and important facts.

_____

_____

_____

_____

Lesson 10 Write Questions Identify facts and details that would be best expressed as an illustration and draw an illustration that aids comprehension.

_____

_____

_____

_____

1. What did you read?
2. What did you learn?
3. What questions do you have?

Lesson 11

1. _____

2. _____

3. _____

Lesson 12

1. _____

2. _____

3. _____

Lesson 13

1. _____

2. _____

3. _____

Lesson 14

1. _____

2. _____

3. _____

Lesson 15

1. _____

2. _____

3. _____

Backyard Safari

Because I live in the city, I rarely see animals that I read about in school. When Dad takes me to the park, I see pigeons and squirrels. Boring! I want to see snakes and rabbits.

Last weekend I stayed with Aunt Marie in the country. Instead of going to the park, I played in Aunt Marie's backyard.

When we arrived at Aunt Marie's, I found her fixing breakfast and wearing a strange hat. "What's that on your head?" I asked.

"It's my safari hat!" She held up a smaller one and tossed it to me. Aunt Marie explained that we were going on a backyard safari.

I inhaled my breakfast. Then we set out toward the yard with binoculars and a magnifying glass.

"Do you hear that?" Aunt Marie asked.

I heard what sounded like a tiny jackhammer. She handed me the binoculars and told me look high up in the tree. I soon found the source of the noise. It was a woodpecker with a red head.

Aunt Marie said that rabbits love to rest under her rose bushes. We lay in the grass and waited. As we waited, she told me all about the critters that call her backyard home—opossum, raccoons, chipmunks, and snakes. Some like to come out early in the morning, others at night.

Then something caught my eye. It was a ball of fur with a nose that was wiggling. "A rabbit," I whispered, even though I wanted to yell. Who knew I could see so much wildlife on a backyard safari!

Gather Evidence Circle two clues from "Backyard Safari" that show the narrator was excited about seeing the animals in Aunt Marie's backyard.

Gather Evidence: Extend Your Ideas Make up a sentence using these clue words to describe a fictional character. Share your sentence with a partner.

_____

_____

Ask Questions Underline three observations the narrator in "Backyard Safari" makes about the animals he or she sees. Now imagine you have the opportunity of talking to an expert about animals that live near humans. What two questions would you ask the expert?

_____

_____

Ask Questions: Extend Your Ideas Look at the observations you underlined. Discuss with a partner what the narrator is able to learn without the help of an expert. What tools does he or she use? Write down what you think you can learn from a backyard safari.

_____

_____

Make Your Case Highlight words from "Backyard Safari" to compare and contrast where the narrator lives and where Aunt Marie lives.

_____

_____

Make Your Case: Extend Your Ideas Briefly explain the similarities and differences between the two places. Then work with a partner and discuss how different the country and city would be if you exchanged the clue words.

Lesson 11

bulb _____

_____

Lesson 12

classify _____

_____

organisms _____

_____

Lesson 13

ingest _____

_____

protista _____

_____

Lesson 14

conduct _____

_____

spores _____

_____

Name _____

Lesson 11 Reread p. 11 of *At the Root of It*. Write a few informative/explanatory paragraphs in which you explain the experiment *in your own words*. What text features can you think of to help explain the experiment?

Lesson 12 Reread p. 7. The author begins describing the six kingdoms with the two bacteria kingdoms. Do you think the author should describe these kingdoms first? Why or why not? Support your answer with evidence from the text.

Lesson 13 Reread the first paragraph on p. 14. Write a response to "Many people with allergies have problems when they come into contact…" Explain what the author might mean by this. Use text evidence to support your answer.

Lesson 14 Reread pp. 16–24 of *Let's Classify Organisms*. Look at the sentence "By organizing groups of plants and animals, scientists are able to learn more about how organisms on Earth are connected and how they grow and change" on pp. 20–21. Have students brainstorm to change this factual statement to a statement of opinion. Then have students read their opinion statements and support their opinions using text evidence.

Lesson 15 Reread *Let's Classify Organisms*. Have students choose from one of the six kingdoms of organisms and ask them to write a short informational paragraph that focuses on the main idea and any important details. Then have students add a sentence to show how this kingdom of organisms is important in the world.

Lesson 12

Using evidence from the text, answer the following questions about
main ideas.

1. Read the first paragraph on page 7. What main idea does the author
   want readers to understand? (Bacteria need to be classified into two
   groups, not one.)

   _____

   _____

2. Which words in the sentence that begins "Scientists have since…"
   help readers understand why scientists wanted to put bacteria into two
   groups?

   _____

   _____

3. Which detail on page 8 tells readers about the shapes of eubacteria?

   _____

   _____

4. Read the second paragraph on page 7 that begins "Archaebacteria
   like…" and the paragraph on page 8. How are the two types of
   bacteria alike? How are they different?

   _____

   _____

5. Which detail on page 10 explains how scientists sort the protist
   kingdom into groups?

   _____

   _____

6. Read page 16. Write the main idea. Then write two details that tell
   about the main idea.

   _____

   _____

Lesson 14

Using evidence from the text, answer the following questions about words that create effect.

1. Read the first sentence on page 16. Which would or words could replace *"look for"* for effect?

   _____

   _____

2. Read page 16. Which two words have a similar meaning to the word *move?*

   _____

   _____

3. Why were these two words used instead of *move?*

   _____

   _____

4. Read the paragraph on page 19. Explain why the word "species" is a better choice than "types" or "kinds" in the sentence.

   _____

   _____

Lesson 11 Articles as Adjectives

Find an article on page 55 in *The Moon Seems to Change*. What is it modifying?

Lesson 12 Use Adjectives

Reread page 4. Identify one of the adjectives used. What does the adjective tell the reader about the noun it modifies?

Lesson 13 Produce a Sentence Using Adjectives

Choose three adjectives from the text. Write a sentence for each.

Lesson 14 Coordinating Conjunctions: Define

Explain how coordinating conjunctions function in a sentence. What are some examples of coordinating conjunctions?

Lesson 15 Coordinating Conjunctions: Word-to-Word

Reread page 12 of the text. Identify a conjunction that connects one word to another and the words it connects.

Lesson 11 Write a Compare/Contrast Essay Highlight important points already addressed in the text and write a concluding statement that offers an opinion.

Lesson 12 Decide on a topic for a newspaper article, gather information by talking to people and using observation skills, perform other research by reading, and plan your articles using a Main Idea graphic organizer.

_____

_____

_____

_____

Lesson 13 Write an Explanatory Text Write a newspaper article using the notes and information you gathered in Lesson 12. Make sure to open the topic with an introductory paragraph and develop the paragraph with facts, definitions, and details.

_____

_____

_____

_____

_____

Lesson 14 Revise the newspaper article to clarify and develop the topic, including facts and details that support the main idea.

_____

_____

_____

_____

_____

Lesson 15 Write a Paragraph Edit your newspaper articles for clarity. Make sure to edit the text to fix spelling and punctuation errors.

_____

_____

_____

_____

_____

1. What did you read?
2. What did you learn?
3. What questions do you have?

Lesson 16

1. _____

2. _____

3. _____

Lesson 17

1. _____

2. _____

3. _____

Lesson 18

1. _____

2. _____

3. _____

Lesson 16

Using evidence from the text, answer the following questions about main idea.

1. What are the topics of each text?

   _____

   _____

2. Which text features are common to both texts to help readers locate information?

   _____

   _____

3. Read page 3 in *At the Root of It* and page 4 in *Let's Classify Organisms*. How are the ways the authors began each text similar?

   _____

   _____

4. In Let's Classify Organisms, read the section Kingdom Plantae that begins on p. 16. What information is included in this section that is not included in *At the Root of It*?

   _____

   _____

5. How are the photos and illustrations similar in both texts? Share examples.

   _____

   _____

   _____

Lesson 16

Using evidence from the text, answer the following questions about word relationships.

1. Read the section "How Roots Absorb Water" on page 8 of At the Root of It. Then read the sentences on page 16 of Let's Classify Organisms that begin "When scientists…" How does the word absorb apply to vascular and non-vascular plants? Explain.

   _____

   _____

   _____

2. Read page 16 in *Let's Classify Organisms* and page 6 in *At the Root of It*. What connection can readers make between the words *vascular* and *nutrients*? Explain.

   _____

   _____

   _____

3. How do the terms *vascular* and *nutrients* apply to people and animals?

   _____

   _____

   _____

4. How are the terms *absorb*, *vascular* and *nutrients* related? How do they apply to other things in the world? Explain.

   _____

   _____

   _____

Lesson 16

vascular plants _____

_____

fungi _____

_____

Lesson 17

quarter _____

_____

archabacteria _____

_____

Lesson 18

trowel _____

_____

grab _____

_____

Name _____

Lesson 16 Reread p. 20 and 21 in *Let's Classify Organisms*. In your opinion, how do text features like the boxed information labeled "Kingdom Animalia" add to the text? Support your opinion with text evidence.

Lesson 17 Reread p. 5 of *At the Root* of It, p. 6 of *Let's Classify Organisms*, and p. 43 of "The Moon Seems to Change." In your opinion, which selection's text features allow you to locate information most efficiently? Be sure to use text evidence to support your answer.

Lesson 18 Reread the first pages of each of the texts. The beginning of each text does not start by explicitly stating its purpose. Instead, they all paint a picture for the reader first. Why do you think the authors chose to begin this way? Support your response with text evidence.

Lesson 17

Using evidence from the text, answer the following questions about text features.

1. Compare the images in each text. Think about the use of photos, illustrations, and diagrams in your response.

   _____

   _____

   _____

   _____

2. Which of the texts had the most useful diagrams for explaining changes over time?

   _____

   _____

3. How are the images in "The Moon Seems to Change" different from the other two texts?

   _____

   _____

   _____

4. Were the images in "The Moon Seems to Change" as effective for presenting the information as the other two texts? Why or why not?

   _____

   _____

   _____

Lesson 16 Coordinating Conjunctions: Phrase-to-Phrase
Reread page 4 of the text. Identify a conjunction that connects one phrase to another and the words it connects.

Lesson 17 Produce a Sentence Using Word-to-Word Coordinating Conjunctions
Write a sentence using word-to-word coordinating conjunctions. Explain why the coordinating conjunction you chose makes sense with the sentence you wrote.

Lesson 18 Produce a Sentence Using Phrase-to Phrase Coordinating Conjunctions
Write a sentence using phrase-to-phrase coordinating conjunctions. Explain why the coordinating conjunction you chose makes sense with the sentence you wrote.

Lesson 16 Write an Opinion Practice presenting your article. Make sure to include illustrations and other text features. Present your article to the class.

_____

_____

_____

_____

_____

_____

_____

Lesson 17 Using what you have learned about a main idea from the reading, conduct brief research, create a sketch, and write two or three questions that closely examine part of nature. Make sure to answer the questions.

_____

_____

_____

_____

_____

_____

_____

Lesson 18 Gather evidence from your research, sort the evidence into the categories provided, and tell how the sorting is relevant to your writing.

_____

_____

_____

_____

_____

_____

_____